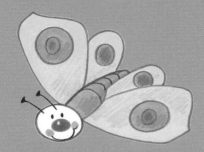

Learn to draw

By the SpiceBox Fun Team

Illustrations by Robert Dyke

Learn to draw

Fifteen easy to follow exercises with step-by-step instructions.

First published in 2007 by
SpiceBox™
1627 Ingleton Ave
Burnaby, BC Canada
www.spicebox.ca

ISBN 1894722531
ISBN 9781894722537

Art Director: Christine Covert
Production: Garett Chan
Illustrator: Robert Dyke
Editorial Direction: Trisha Pope

contents

Hi! My name is Bill the Bear.
Do you want to learn how to draw? I can teach
you. Just follow the steps in this book and you can
draw all kinds of things. Do not worry if your
picture looks a little different from the ones that
you see here, just have fun drawing and coloring,
and use your imagination!

Bill the bear

We will start by drawing the cutest, most adorable, friendliest, cuddliest, all around most amazing teddy bear — me! Follow the steps and then try drawing me walking or sitting.

Draw a large circle for my body and a smaller one on top for my head

Add my ears, nose, mouth, eyes and a ribbon

Step 3

Add my arms

Step 4

Add my feet

Step 5

Color me in!

thanks for drawing me!

As you become better at drawing, you can let your imagination run free… Practice drawing each exercise in this book and think about combining characters, or making them do different things.

9

Bonnie the butterfly

Now let's try to draw my good friend Bonnie the butterfly. You can change the colors of a butterfly to any color you like. Butterflies can have an amazing variety of colors on their wings. Can you remember the last time you saw a butterfly?

Draw a sausage shape for the body and a small circle for the head

Add wings

10

Add eyes, mouth, nose and antennae

Color in your butterfly

Add circle shapes on wings

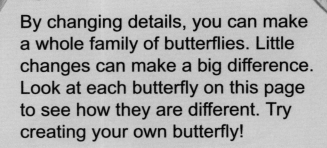

By changing details, you can make a whole family of butterflies. Little changes can make a big difference. Look at each butterfly on this page to see how they are different. Try creating your own butterfly!

Douglas the dog

I know a dog named Douglas who is a very excitable puppy, always running, wriggling, and playing. He would be fun to draw if he would ever hold still long enough that you could draw him. Quickly, before he gets distracted, draw him out following these steps. After you are done, try drawing him in action!

Step 1

Draw a large circle for the body and a smaller one on top for the head, add a ribbon

Step 2

Add a nose, a mouth and some eyes

Step 3

Add ears and feet

Step 4

Add a tail and patch under his chin

Step 5

Add spots and color Douglas in

Look at Douglas and the snail! Dogs are always very curious. What are you curious about? Why don't you try to draw it too?

13

CharLie the Cat

Douglas the dog loves to play with and chase Charlie the cat. Charlie is just as energetic as Douglas, so if you want to draw Charlie you better work fast. Like all kittens, he loves to play with a ball of yarn.

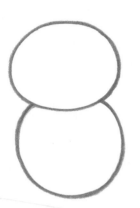

Draw a large circle for the body and a smaller one on top for the head

Add ears, a nose, the mouth, and eyes

14

Step 3

Add a ribbon and legs

Step 4

Add a tail and some whiskers

Step 5

Add a patch of fur under his chin

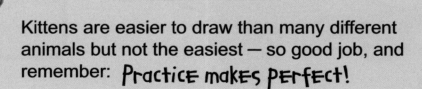

Kittens are easier to draw than many different animals but not the easiest — so good job, and remember: **Practice makes perfect!**

freddie the fish

Charlie the Cat has one favorite food and it is fish. The fish on this page know that Charlie is looking for dinner so I do not think they will slow down! Follow these steps to make a fish:

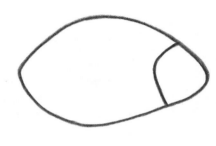

Draw an oval shape for the body and then draw in the head shape

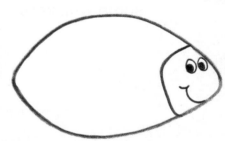

Add eyes and a mouth

step 3

Add a top fin and the tail

step 5

Color in Freddie the fish

step 4

Add two bottom fins

Tropical fish are some of the world's most colorful creatures so make sure you let your colors fly. The name for a group of fish is a school — can you draw a school of different looking fish?

Sailboat

If you can draw a boat, you can catch a fish from the deep blue sea. On these pages, you can see how to draw different sorts of boats.

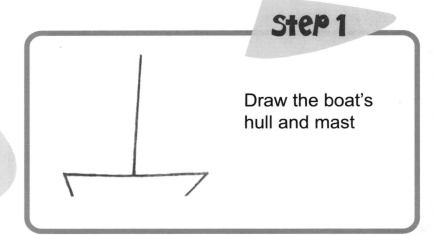

Draw the boat's hull and mast

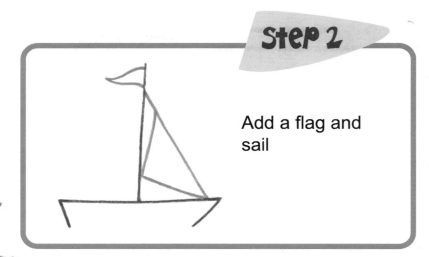

Add a flag and sail

Step 3

Add another sail

Step 5

Color in your sailboat

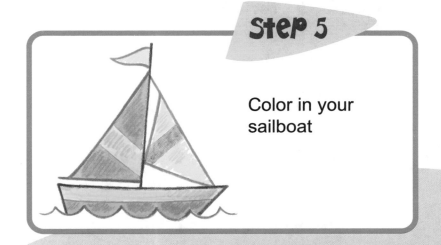

Step 4

Add a wavy sea

Steamboats move all on their own, without needing help from the wind. Follow the instructions for drawing a sailboat and replace the sail with a steam stack if you want to make a steamboat.

Airplane

ZOOOOOM! The fastest way to move is in an airplane. No boat can match a plane for speed. Use the following steps to go up and away on an airplane.

Step 1

Draw a sausage shape for the body and then add wings

Step 2

Add a tail and an engine

Step 3

Add wheels
and the
pilot's cabin

Step 5

Color in your
airplane

Step 4

Add windows
for the
passengers

Jets are the fastest planes but old-fashioned propeller planes are fun too. Imagine the sounds each kind makes.

which one do you think would make the most noise?

super cars

Everyday people drive cars and trucks to get to work or do errands. Cars are not as fast as airplanes but they can still motor! **VROOOOM!**

Draw body shape and add a half circle, on top

Add wheels and windows

Step 3

Add a bumper
and headlight

Step 4

Add doors
and a grill

Step 5

Color in your
super car

Notice how the front of the car looks like it is smiling?
The headlights are like eyes and the grill is the mouth.
Try drawing your car with a surprised expression, or a
sleepy one.

Can you draw anything to bring it to life?

circus clowns

How many clowns do you think you could fit into a car? It might be hard to get very many into a car because clowns are always joking, acting silly, and playing games…

Draw a circle for the body and a smaller circle on top for the head

Add a hat and arms

Add hands, a nose, a mouth and eyes

Add a frilly collar and big feet

Color in the circus clown

Can you draw a juggling clown or one who is walking on a tightrope? Clowns work at the circus with elephants and lions and can do amazing tricks.

What other tricks can you imagine a clown doing?

MELODY MOUSE

Every clown knows the one thing that a giant elephant fears — a tiny mouse! Meet Melody the mouse. Even though she is so small, she would make the biggest elephant terrified! You aren't afraid of Melody are you?

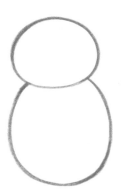

Draw a large circle for the body and a smaller one on top for the head

Add big mouse ears, a nose, a mouth and eyes

Step 3

Add arms and feet

Step 4

Add whiskers and tail

Step 5

Color Melody in

Can you imagine any other scenes for Melody the mouse? Draw her with other animals, except for maybe Charlie the cat who likes to chase mice!

27

Derek the Duck

Derek the duck is not an ugly duckling at all! Can you draw Derek? When drawing animals try and imagine the sound they make and imitate it. What sound does a duckling make?

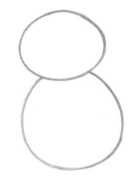

Draw a large circle for the body and a smaller one on top for the head

Step 2

Add a beak, two eyes and two wings

STEP 3

Add two feet

STEP 5

Color in Derek the duck

STEP 4

Add a tail and crest

Ducks can swim and can fly, and you can draw Derek doing both. A duckling is a bird that hatches from an egg. Can you draw Derek the duckling as a very young baby?

Can you draw and decorate an egg?

29

connie the cow

What do cows put on their sandwiches? Moosterd & Cowchep! Try drawing Connie the cow and use different colors for her spots.

Draw a large circle for the body and a smaller oval for the face, add a head shape on top

Add eyes, a mouth, nose and two horns

30

Add two ears
and some feet

Add spots
and color in
Connie the
cow

Add a tail

One of the cows has a bell — why
do you think a cow would need to
wear a cowbell? What holiday do
you suppose is Connie's favorite?
Why Moo Years Day, of course!

31

Hazel the Witch

When fall approaches and the leaves in the trees change color you know it will soon be time for Halloween — time for Hazel the witch to take flight with her broom!

32

Add a mouth, hands and some shoes

Add hair, stars, moons and a her broom

Color Hazel in

Witches can do all kinds of magic spells. Try and make different looking witches and make sure you don't make identical twins, otherwise you won't be able to tell which witch is which!

Stuart the Snowman

Once it is fall, and Halloween, it will soon be winter. Stuart the snowman is happy when it is cold because he won't melt away. Stuart owns a collection of different hats to help him brave those really cold December days.

Draw a circle for the body and a smaller circle on top for the head

Add a hat, a carrot nose and eyes

34

STEP 3

Add a button mouth and two arms

STEP 5

Color in Stuart the snowman

STEP 4

Add feet and three buttons

What kind of toothpick does Stuart use? an ice-pick!

Stuart the snowman wears a different scarf, and can have different colored eyes made of buttons. Make sure to keep him cold, or he will turn into a puddle!

Buddy the bunny

You know it is spring when you see an Easter bunny.

Draw a large circle for the body and a smaller one on top for the head

Add eyes, nose, mouth and two long bunny ears

36

Step 3

Add arms and two feet

Step 4

Add whiskers and a tail

Step 5

Color in your bunny

Buddy the bunny knocked on my door and I asked who's there? He said "Some Bunny." "Some bunny who?" I replied. "Some bunny is eating all your Easter candy!" What a silly bunny!

37

Have fun drawing!

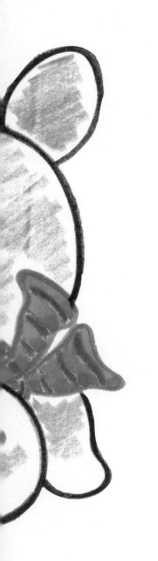

First published in 2007 by
SpiceBox™
1627 Ingleton Ave
Burnaby, BC Canada
www.spicebox.ca